A Guide for Home Buyers

Valerie Hockert, Editor

Valerie Hockert, Editor
CollProf@aol.com

Table of Contents

Introduction

This book is a collection of articles that were written as individual reports for the home buyer. After reading the entire book, you should be well-equipped to purchase that new home. Happy house hunting!

Valerie Hockert

Typical Home Buyers' Questions

By Cherie Shoemaker, CRS, GRI

The home-buying process can be complicated or it can be extremely easy. Mostly, it depends on how informed you are about financial options, area considerations and deed restrictions. You may choose to find an experienced real estate agent who will take you through the process.) Typically, the home-buying consumer has many questions that come to mind. A few of the most asked questions follow.

Should We Buy a Home Now?

Of course, the answer is yes! The reason is simple. Prices of new or previously owned homes continue to increase in price. Delaying the purchase of a home allows prices and interest rates to go higher. Interest rates are never the same, as they go up or down according to the constant change in the money market. Over-all, interest rates have steadily increased over the past 35 years. By buying now, you can realize a lower price. If interest rates did increase substantially during the process, you have a couple of options. One, you could always refinance at a later date. Two, you could consider an adjustable-rate mortgage which starts with a low interest rate, and then goes up or down at the anniversary date. This is a good choice because your payments would be lower in the first part of the loan, wherein you pay the largest amount of interest or a temporary buy-down, much like an ARM but have "stepped-up" interest rates with a known end rate.

By buying now you would begin to build equity. Equity is defined as the amount of cash that you have when you eventually sell your home, after you have paid all the mortgage and any claims against your property have been satisfied. In other words, this is the profit you will receive when you sell your home. This is the way people are able to move up to a better home, as they will have more down payment to invest. Most mortgage lenders have programs that start with as little as 3% of the total price of a home. Besides the down payment investment, you will also need money for closing costs and prepaid items.

Is There a Rule of Thumb Used by Lending Institutions to Determine How Much Mortgage We Can Afford?

How much you can afford depends on your family income and your credit rating. The guidelines that need to be used are suggested by the Federal National Mortgage Association (called FNMA-FANNIE MAE). FNMA is a privately owned association which has a pool of investors who buy packages of loans from the banks and mortgage companies that originate mortgages. FNMA is regulated by the government and they set the guidelines for mortgage loans. Currently your mortgage payment, which is principle, interest, taxes and insurance (PITI) should not exceed 28% of your family's gross monthly income. This is called your top ratio. The bottom ratio is figured on your monthly house payment plus all monthly debts. This figure should not exceed 36% of your income. If a debt can be paid off in ten months and it is not over $100 monthly then that debt will not be counted against you as you put more down, these ratios can be expanded.

Monthly Affordability Indexed on 28% Income

Monthly Income	Monthly Payment
30000	850
3400	952
3800	1064
4000	1120
4500	1260
5000	1400
5500	1540
6000	1680

Monthly Loan Amortization Payments

An amortization table showing the amounts of monthly payments required to retire the principal and pay the interest for five different loans for a 30-day period.

Loan	8%	9.75%	10%
$70,000	$514	$599	$693
$80,000	$587	$687	$702
$100,000	$734	$860	$878
$120,000	$881	$1032	$1054
$140,000	$1,027	$1,204	$1,230

How Can I Be Prequalified For a Loan?

This is the first step taken, even before you start to preview homes. It's important to find out what price home you can afford to buy. The loan officer will set up a meeting with no obligation to you. The loan officer will ask you a number of questions and discuss the following information: The amount of monthly income, length of time on the job, a list of all assets and all debts, and account numbers for both. Be completely honest with the loan officer. If you have had credit problems, discuss this with the loan officer. There are many cases where those with past credit problems can still be approved for a loan. It does depend on the circumstances. Lenders are sticklers about good credit, so at this time you should have a credit check run. This costs about $50 to $75. It is better to know in advance if there is anything on your credit record that could keep you from being approved for a loan. Your loan officer can tell you what to do to clean up any credit problem. The source of your down payment will be verified.

The best part of being prequalified is that you may ask your loan officer to write a letter indicating that you are prequalified for a certain loan amount. When you have found your home, your offer will carry more credibility with a seller if accompanied by a letter from a lender. This can work in your favor if there are other buyers biding against you.

What Are Discount Points?

Discount points are fees to compensate the lender for making a loan at a lower than market rate. The amount of discount points depends on the money-market conditions, the credit of the borrower, and the rate and term of the note. One point equals 1% of the loan amount.

Why Must We Pay an Origination Fee?

This fee is charged to the borrower by the lender as compensation for originating a new loan. Normally, the origination fee is equal to 1% of the loan amount. These fees help the lender for the normal overhead of running a mortgage company: paying the loan officer, checking credit reports and title reports, paying an underwriter, office equipment and supplies, etc.

Is It Always Necessary to Have an Inspection Report of the Property?

It could be a good idea. The inspector does a thorough inspection of all of the major components of the property. The inspector will explain to you the regular maintenance and upkeep you should have on this home. If there are too many hidden problems, you have the option of not buying this particular property; or you can negotiate with the seller to make some, or all, of the repairs. Even if you are buying a new home, it might be wise to be sure that the construction is completed as stated in the contract signed by the builder.

Why Should We Work With a Real Estate Agent?

You could go through the real estate classified section and find ads that appeal to you, then call several real estate offices. You may think the property sounds perfect for you, only to discover after driving to a particular neighborhood that you couldn't possibly live there, or that the property condition turns you away. Often you might spend a good deal of time and still not find the special home that is perfect for your family.

If this does not appeal to you, you may consider making an appointment with an experienced real estate agent for a consultation session. Discuss your desires, area preferences, preferred style of home and amenities. At the agent's office you will have access to the entire Multiple Listing Service (MLS), which covers all the properties listed in your area. Together you can select the homes you want to see. The agent will set the appointments and in a short time you could be selecting the home of your choice. Relying on the expertise of an agent may be your best choice in order to avoid needless problems in the complex world of real estate.

"Pre-Approval" Can Help You Buy Your Dream House

By Mary Ann Lawford

You really aren't ready to look for a house until you know how much house you can afford. Looking at homes you *can't* afford leads to disappointment, and puts a damper on what should be a happy experience.

A visit with a bank of mortgage company should be your first step once you begin to think about buying a home. Sometimes you will find out from a banker that you can afford *more* than you thought you could.

Make a few phone calls to local lending institutions, such as savings and loans, banks, or mortgage brokers to find out whether there are special state or federal loan programs available to you that will offer better terms than conventional loans. There are various federal programs such as FHA, VA, and Community Home Buyers, and many states have special programs for first time buyers, buyers in rural areas, or buyers in certain redevelopment areas in some cities. These special plans often offer lower interest rates or have more lenient credit or income guidelines than conventional loan programs.

Initially you should call several different types of lenders. If you are working with a real estate agent, you should ask that person to recommend a loan agent. However, don't limit yourself...call several. For home purchase loans, mortgage brokers and savings and loan institutions usually offer more varied and better loan programs than banks, which typically deal more in consumer loans and refinancing on homes. If you belong to a credit union, call them. Some credit unions make home-purchase loans, but often they do not have access to the special government loan programs. Call at least three mortgage brokers. Mortgage brokers have access to many types of lenders: banks, savings and loans, insurance companies, investment groups, etc. Not all mortgage brokers have access to the government programs that you may be eligible for, and some less-than-scrupulous lenders will offer you the loan that makes them the most money instead of the one that is best for you. That is why I suggest calling three.

It's a good idea to meet with more than one loan agent, once you have narrowed down your search on the telephone to determine which will work best for you and with you. When you meet with him, be prepared with copies of your paycheck stubs (usually one months' worth) and W-w forms (two years), all of your debt information and, if possible, a copy of your credit report. You can usually obtain a copy of your credit report from a local credit reporting agency for a small fee (usually under $20). Look in the yellow pages under "credit reporting" to see if there is an agency near you. Having this information will enable the loan agents to give you the best estimate of how much you can qualify for. It's important that you get precise information from all of the loan agents about all of the charges that will be involved in obtaining a loan from them. These charges can vary greatly. There are companies who quote low rates but have a lot of "add-on" fees. Get a written estimate of all the charges. In some cases, some of the fees associated with the loan can be added into the loan amount, thereby reducing the amount of cash you have to come up with to buy your home.

Once you have found a loan company of bank you're happy with, the next step is actually getting "approved." There is a big difference between pre-qualified" and "pre-approved." Pre-qualified means that the loan company has looked at your information but has not formally verified any of it and is not making any commitment to lend you money. A pre-qualification letter is usually so full of holes it is virtually useless except as a very basic guideline as to what one can afford.

Being "pre-approved" is entirely different. To get pre-approved, you will fill out a formal loan application and supply the lenders with all of the information requested. They will verify your employment by sending your employer a document to fill out stating that you are employed there, and stating what your wages are, and whether your employment is expected to continue. They will order a credit report, usually from all three of the major reporting companies and will verify with your bank that you have sufficient funds on deposit for your down payment and closing costs. If you don't have all of the money, or if some of it is coming from a parent as a gift, you will be asked to document that information. You may be asked for tax returns as well as your W-2's. You may also be asked for a letter of explanation if there are any late payments or derogatory items on your credit report. If you have obtained a copy of your credit report before going to a lender, and there are any items that are derogatory, or late items, you should immediately challenge any items which you fell may be in error. If you write to the credit reporting agency and dispute the validity of any items, they are required to verify it with the company who made the derogatory report—in writing. If the credit agency requests verification and does not receive it within 30 days, they must, by law, remove that item. It is in your best interest to dispute any derogatory item on your credit report. If you cannot get these items removed, it is helpful if you have a reasonable excuse for them. If you have been involved in a divorce in which your ex-spouse is or was responsible for any of the debts, they will want to see a copy of the divorce decree. Your credit rating has a direct bearing on whether or not you can get a loan and what your interest rate will be, so it is vitally important to have it as clean as possible.

After all of the documentation is collected, they will actually submit your application to the underwriting department or loan committee for consideration. By the time this occurs, your loan agent has a pretty good idea whether or not you can get the loan, so this submission is mostly a formality. There may be some conditions or requirements given by the underwriters for your approval, but these are usually just supportive documents regarding your employment, letters regarding credit, or some other small items. When you get a final "approval," the only condition will be that the home you choose is appraised for the sale price and meets the standards of the lender or the government program issuing the loan.

The "approved status puts you, as a buyer, in the best possible negotiating position and ensures that when you find your "dream house" you will, indeed, be able to buy it. When you are ready to make an offer on the home you choose, you will be offering the seller "a sure thing." They will know that they don't have to wait three or four weeks wondering if the sale will go through. "Pre-approval" also makes it much easier when you are trying to negotiate a lower sale price, asking for other concessions, or if there is more than one offer on the house. In any of these situations the "pre-approved" buyer will almost certainly win out.

Being "pre-approved" is a win-win tactic. It takes time and leg work but the results are worth the effort. Buying a home is a stressful and emotional process. Being prepared and informed is the best way to reduce the stress and to keep those emotions "happy" ones, as they should be.

Guidelines to Home Mortgages

By Cherie Shoemaker, CRS, GRI

In today's mortgage-lending, lenders apply guidelines established by FNMA, FHA, VA, and secondary investors to determine an applicant's ability to make good on a mortgage obligation. There are also guidelines for assessing the condition of the house that you buy. It may have to be brought up to date and repaired to qualify.

As a buyer you should understand the terms, conditions, and the various types of mortgages available in the market place. Also, having a knowledge of the guidelines involved will give you an advantage in buying or selling real estate. The following guidelines are for conventional loans, FHA, and VA loans Maximum loan limits are determined by your local area and vary according to the type of loan.

Guidelines for Conventional Loans

The Guidelines for LTV: (Loan to Value) for single family properties for a conventional loan is 95% to 97% for fixed-rate owner-occupied principal residence, 90% to 95% LTV for adjustable-rate owner occupied, 70% to 90% for second-home refinance, 70% to 80% for investment property, and 90% for two-family properties, owner-occupied.

Co-Borrowers: If the LTV is greater than 90%, a co-borrower must owner-occupy the property when his/her income is used for qualifying. 95% LTV if primary borrower qualifies for payment at 35/43 ratio on his or her own income. However, if the LTV is 90% or less, the co-borrower need not occupy the property. In addition, the co-borrower will no longer be required to be a family member or have a personal relationship with the borrower as long as that person is not an interested party in the transaction (e.g., seller, builder, realtor).

Resident Aliens: The maximum LTV for non-permanent resident aliens has been increased to 75% (except for FHA). In addition, this type of buyer no longer needs to place a specified amount of funds into an escrow account of the term of the mortgage.

Buydown: No buydown will be allowed on investor purchases. Also, buydown funds may not be returned to the borrower if the borrower pays off the mortgage. Borrower can qualify up to 2% below the note rate.

Bankruptcy: A bankruptcy must have been discharged for two years prior to closing for a buyer to be considered, or the circumstances must have been such that it was not the borrower's fault. The buyer must also have established new, good credit during this two-year period of time.

Private Mortgage Insurance: Mortgage insurance is an insurance policy provided by a third-party company to assume a portion of the risk of a mortgage loan for the lender upon default by the buyer. Private Mortgage insurance (PMI) is a requirement on all loans with a loan to value greater than 80%. You will have an initial payment at the closing of the property and a monthly payment thereafter. You will be give the rates at the time of loan application. Refund of the PMI: If the borrower builds 20% or more in equity, or upon selling or payoff of the loan, the borrower may request that a prorated portion of these funds be returned.

Guidelines for FHA Loans

FHA (Federal Housing Administration) is mandated to be a self-supporting agency by means of income derived from an insurance charge commonly referred to as MIP (Mortgage Insurance Premium). The up-front fee is 2.25% plus 1/2% annually of the base loan amount. This amount can be financed in the loan or paid in cash at the time of the closing.

Borrowed Down Payment: Permissible if loan is secured. It cannot be a signature loan and borrower must qualify for both payments.

Second Lien: A second lien is allowed under the following conditions: 1) The first and second mortgages combined do not exceed the loan to value and the maximum loan amount for a first lien; 2) The borrower qualifies with both payments; 3) The second loan does not contain a balloon payment due before five years; 4) The second loan must have payments that are substantially level; and 5) There is no prepayment penalty.

Buydown: Temporary buydowns are permissible; however, seller contributions are limited to 6% of the sales price. The borrower will be underwritten and must qualify at 2% below the note rate on a 2-1 and 3-2-1 buydown.

Investor Loans: As of December, 1989, FHA will no longer accept loans on investment properties.

Assumptions: For all mortgages that were or will be endorsed after November 7, 1989, HUD now requires a review of the credit worthiness (income minus debt) of each person who seeks to assume an FHA mortgage.

Prepayment Penalty: FHA loans may be prepaid without a penalty. For loans committed prior to August 2, 1985, 30 days' written notice of intention to prepay is required. Failure to do so may result in an additional 30 days' interest being charged to the payoff. Interest is collected in arrears on FHA loans.

Acceptability of Credit Risk: A borrower who is presently delinquent on any federal debt (e.g., HUD Insured mortgage, student loan, SBA loan, etc.) or has a judgment lien against the property for a debt owed to the United States is not eligible until the account is brought current, or satisfactory arrangements have been made with the federal agency, or the judgment has been paid.

12

Power of Attorney: A Power of Attorney may be used but only under limited circumstances, such as when a co-borrower is out of the country. It must be specific power of attorney and it has to be approved by the lender and the title company. It cannot be used for the borrower signature on the mortgage application.

Appraised Value: Appraised value always means the lesser of acquisition cost or appraised value plus closing costs.

Co-borrower: 1) If co-borrowers are unrelated, the maximum loan to value is 75% of the appraised value. 2) When there is an identity of interest between borrower and seller (e.g., any family relationship or corporation selling to employee) the maximum loan to value is 85%. Exceptions are children buying parents' principal residence, or an employee of a builder buying a home for a principal residence. These buyers are eligible for maximum loan amounts.

Gift Letter: Permissible if from direct family member. A letter from the family member is required stating the amount, relationship to borrower, and the borrower's name, address and phone number. It must also state that the gift is not to be repaid.

Co-Signer on a Non-Mortgage Loan: If the borrower is a co-signer on a non-mortgage loan (such as a car note, etc.) the debt will be counted unless all of the following apply: 1) Statements from both parties that the co-signer never has made any of the payments; 2) Copies of canceled checks showing that the other party has made all the last 12 months' payments; and 3) All payments have been made on time.

Foreclosure or Deed-in-Lieu of Foreclosure: If, within the last three years, HUD paid an insurance claim on behalf of the borrower on a prior insured mortgage or had a VA-guaranteed or conventional mortgage foreclosure or deed-in-lieu of, then the borrower is ineligible for an insured mortgage, unless the action was a result of well-defined, extenuating circumstances beyond the borrower's control.

Bankruptcy: A bankruptcy may have been caused by business conditions or other circumstances beyond the control of the borrowers and should not be constructed as an adverse element in the borrowers' attitude toward obligations if: 1) A satisfactory credit standing has been re-established over a period of at least one year after discharge of the bankruptcy; 2) No new derogatory information is reported; and 3) The borrower has arranged his/her affairs to preclude the need for credit purposes.

Sources of Funds for Closing: In most cases, a cash-on-hand letter is not acceptable. Funds must be deposited and verified. The cash on hand that is needed is usually two to three months of monthly payment besides closing funds.

Guidelines for VA Mortgages
VA Funding Fee: This can be paid by the seller or Veteran or it may be added to the mortgage

amount. Rates will be quoted at the time of mortgage application.

Certificate of Eligibility: In order to obtain a Certificate of Eligibility, the following is required: 1) All separation papers (DD-214); 2) Statement of service from commanding officer if the veteran is on active duty; and 3) VA form 1880 completed and signed by the veteran.

Assumptions: As of March 1, 1988, a VA loan is not assumable without prior approval of VA or authorized agent. The prospective purchaser must assume full liability for repayment of the loan, including the indemnity liability to the VA, and qualify from a credit standpoint. The assumptee will be required to pay a funding fee equal to 0.5% of the loan balance. A processing fee may be charged by the loan holder for determining credit worthiness of the assumee.

Restoration of Entitlement: This may be requested if the loan is paid in full, or if the loan is assumed by another eligible veteran who substitutes his entitlement for the entitlement used by the original veteran.

Buydown: Temporary buydowns are allowed, but credit underwriting will be based on full payment amount. The buydown may be considered to offset short term obligations. The escrowed buydown funds may not revert to the builder/seller under any circumstances. If the property is sold subject to, or, on an assumption of the loan, the escrow must continue to pay out on behalf of the new owner.

This is only a partial listing of guidelines under the three types of mortgages. If you have questions concerning particular circumstances not mentioned you may call a real estate agent or mortgage loan officer.

What You Need to Apply for a Mortgage

By Beth Anne Serepca

As you may have already discovered, buying a house is a major project! Exhaustive amounts of paperwork, as well as the huge commitment of your time, energy and money can seem overwhelming. To keep things as easy and stress-free as possible, start keeping immaculate records of your finances *now,* whether you plan to apply for a mortgages in two weeks or six months. This way, when the time comes, everything you'll need will be right at your fingertips.

Basically, a bank or mortgage company wants to know about your income, assets, debt, and credit history. This helps them determine the risk of lending you money, how much to lend, as well as your ability and willingness to pay it back in a timely manner.

Although the lender will send for your credit report, it is a good idea to obtain a copy for yourself beforehand to make sure there are no mistakes, and to fix any credit problems *before* you apply for a mortgage. You can request one from the credit bureau Equifax (1-800-685-1111) for $3 to $8 (depending on where you live), or from a "credit reporting agency" in your local Yellow Pages.

Following is a list of documents, lenders will want. It may seem long, but not every item will apply to you:

- Check(s) for the application and credit report fee.
- Signed copy of the real estate purchase contract.
- Signed copy of the sales contract (if you are selling your current home).
- Copies of two most current pay stubs (showing year-to-date earnings and social security number) to cover most recent 30-day pay period.
- Two-year history of employment, including names and addresses
- Tax returns and W-2 forms for the past two years.
- Copies of statements from all bank accounts for the past three months.
- Two-year history of residency (addresses and dates)
- 12 months canceled rent payment checks
- Landlord's name and address
- Outstanding loan and credit card balances and monthly payments (copies of the most recent statement or coupon book), including address and account numbers.
- Copy of auto title (is car is owned and is less than five years old).
- Transcript or diploma (if you were a student in the past two years).

- Copy of 401K/IRA/Keogh/Profit Sharing plan (if applicable)
- Copy of divorce decree and separation (if applicable).
- Copy of driver's license
- Copy of Social Security card (FHA) only).
- Year-to-Date Profit or Loss Statement and current Balance Sheet (if self-employed).
- Certificate of DD214 and original certificate of eligibility (VA only)
- Bankruptcy papers (if applicable)
- Award letter and copy of most recent check (if you receive disability, social security, or retirement).
- Letter of explanation (if there are late payments or defaults on your credit report, or if you recently experienced a period of unemployment.
- Letter of expectation (if you expect a raise, promotion, bonuses, or any other increase of income in the near future).

Taking the Frustration out of Applying for Mortgages

By Rodney D. Young

Many first time homebuyers have had the fun of purchasing a new home tainted by the overwhelming process required by their lending institution to complete the mortgage loan application. But this process need not become so intimidating.

While the mounts of paperwork the lender requests may, at least on the surface, seem unimportant or even personal, the lender seldom requests documentation without a pertinent reason. The easiest way to keep a potential homebuyer from becoming frustrated by the lending process is to simply explain what to expect from the very start.

Credit History

The lender will begin by examining the buyer's credit history with particular emphasis on the last two years. The borrower may expect to write letters explaining any late payments appearing in this period, and may have to write explanations regarding late payments from even earlier dates. While it is sometimes difficult to recall why a payment was mailed late over two years ago, it is important that the buyer at least demonstrate an effort to comply with the lender's request. If the borrower discloses in any of his or her letters that a divorce occurred, he or she will be expected to supply a file-stamped (that is a recorded) copy of the divorce decree and marriage settlement agreement.

In examining the credit, the lender will verify at minimum the last twelve months' rental history with the borrower's current property manager, or look carefully at nay preceding mortgage history within the last twelve months. It is, therefore, expedient to provide to the lender upfront the name, address and telephone number of any property manager for the last 12 months, or to provide the name and account number of any mortgage within the previous 12 months.
I
If the borrower has experienced bankruptcy within the last three to five years, a detailed letter explaining the circumstances of the bankruptcy is necessary, as well as a file-stamped copy of the discharge and the schedules filed. If the bankruptcy occurred at least five to ten years prior to the application, the discharge and schedules will probably not be necessary; but a letter explaining the circumstances will most likely be requested.

Assets

The lender does more, however, than simply examine the borrower's past credit history in making a determination regarding a mortgage loan application. The lender will also look very carefully at assets. Assets do more than show that the borrower has sufficient funds to close a real estate loan, although this is the primary purpose. Assets may aid the borrower to qualify for a mortgage with a payment relatively high compared to his or her income. In some instances the lender may request copies of the borrower's most recent 401K statement for that very purpose.

The most important documentation a lender will ask for when verifying assets are copies of the most recent, consecutive bank statements covering a three-month period. The lender will carefully examine the statements to insure that the borrower's address matches the address disclosed on the application, that no large deposits which cannot be accounted for by the borrower's income appear on the statement, and that no remarks regarding checks written for insufficient funds appear on the statements. If any large deposits do appear, the borrower will be asked to provide a written explanation and to document the source of funds. For instance, if the borrower explains that he sold a car, he should provide a copy of the bill of sale to the lender. Letters explaining any charges for insufficient funds will also be expected by the lender. If the borrower does not provide the bank statements in a timely manner, the lender may send a verification of deposit to the borrower's banking institution. The disadvantage of this, however, is that the banking institution may have a turn-around time of several weeks before returning the document to the lender.

Employment

Similarly, the borrower's employment may be documented by a written verification of employment. The employer, however, like the banking institution, has no real interest in whether the borrower obtains a mortgage or not, and so may take several weeks to return the verification. Therefore, it is in the borrower's best interest to provide to the lender pay stubs covering the most recent 30-day period, and W-2 Forms for the most recent two years. Using this information and a verbal statement from the employer, the lender may proceed with documenting the borrower's stable employment. The lender will carefully examine the pay stubs to determine whether any deductions (other than ordinary ones) appear. If, for instance, the lender discovers s deduction that isn't standard, a letter explaining it will be requested. In this way, the lender may determine whether a loan through an employer or against a 401K plan exists. If the borrower has not been employed for at least two years at his current job, he or she must provide on the application the names of their other employers so that they may be contacted to verify previous employment. If there is a "gap of employment" for more than a one-month period in the previous two years, the lender will request a written explanation of the gap.

To verify the income and employment of the self-employed borrower, or the borrower who has investment property, the lender will often ask for the previous two years' tax returns with all applicable schedules and attachments, as well as a year-to-date profit and loss statement and balance sheet. Self-employed borrowers (or borrowers employed by a family business) should prepare themselves for this inevitability. Also, borrowers with an interest exceeding 25% in a partnership, S-corporation, or corporation, will be expected to provide not only tax returns, but corporate returns or partnership returns for the previous two years.

Summary

In short, to expedite processing f the mortgage-loan application and prevent frustration of the new homeowner, he or she should be prepared to provide to the lender:

1. Explanations of late payments, bankruptcies, and any significant debt not disclosed on the application.
2. Bank statements covering the most recent consecutive three-month period and explanations of any large deposits or insufficient-funds charges.
3. Pay stubs covering the most recent 30-day period and explanations for any out-of-the-ordinary deductions appearing thereon.
4. W-2 forms covering the most recent two-year period.
5. File-stamped copies of bankruptcy discharges and schedules, divorce decrees and marriage settlement agreements.
6. Copies of personal tax returns for the previous two years.
7. Copies of corporate or partnership tax returns for the previous two years.
8. A year-to-date profit and loss statement and balance sheet.

This list might seem more than a little intimidating to the potential homebuyer, but an awareness that this is what the lender might ask to see prior to making the loan application will soften the blow and make the transition from potential buyer to new homeowner an easy and rewarding one.

Where Does Your Loan Application Go After Completion?

By Charles W. Legeman, JD

You have completed all of the documents that your loan agent gave you, including the loan application also known as the 1003 form, your verification of deposits (VOD), verification of employment (VOE), verification of mortgage or rent (VOM), a credit authorization, and submitted three months' bank statements, as well as two years' federal income tax returns or two years' W2's showing your income. Where does it all go when submitted?

1. The loan agent will give your package to a loan processor in his office. The loan processor will first review the application, which should have a list of addresses of where you have lived over the past two years, where you have worked over the past two years, your current address and current employer. You will also need to list your bank accounts, any other assets you may have, such as stocks, bonds, mutual funds, 401K plans or IRA's. You will also need to provide all of your debt, such as credit card accounts, mortgages, car loans, student loans, etc.

2. Once the loan processor has reviewed the application, he or she will then send all of the verifications to the various institutions to confirm that what you have submitted is true, as stated on the documents. The loan agent will also get a credit report from a credit reporting agency showing all of your debt, present and past, including credit card, mortgage, and car payments, and how timely you are making monthly payments and also whether or not the debt has been paid or charged off because of bankruptcy or inability to pay. Some lending institution will disqualify you immediately if you have had two late mortgage payments in the past year, too many late payments on credit card or auto loans, or if you have filed a bankruptcy in the past two years.

3. Once the loan processor has received all of the confirming data and information from all of the above, the loan agent will review the data against what you have provided on your application. If there are any discrepancies, the loan processor will notify the loan agent, who will contact you the borrower, and ask you to provide letters of explanations as to the discrepancies.

4. Once you have delivered the letters and the processor has what he or she would consider a complete file, tree copies, also known as packages, of your file, will be distributed to an underwriter, senior loan officer, and the loan agent.

The underwriter will then check your income against expenses and review your credit report to see if you qualify for any of the loans offered by that particular institution. Underwriters for conventional lending institutions do not like to see expenses, including the mortgage payment, exceed 40% of your gross monthly income. There are non-traditional institutions and private parties that will allow expenses over 40%. If you fall into that category, your mortgage broker can help you find those sources.

The underwriter will also review your past two years' tax returns and W2s. If there has been a large increase or decrease in your income, they may want a letter of explanation as to why there was a change in the income. They will also ask for letters of explanation for a late mortgage payment, late credit card payments or late car payments.

The underwriter will check your savings or checking accounts for the past three months to verify that your down payment is shown and to also verify that you have adequate reserves (reflecting savings equal to two to six months' income) that will enable you to pay your bills should you have a sudden change in your job.

Once the underwriter has completed his or her work, it will be sent to a senior loan officer or loan committee, depending upon the lending institution and its size. The senior loan officer will review the file and consult with the loan agent and the underwriter and/or other senior loan officers, if a loan committee is involved, and either approve or disapprove the loan.

This approval process can take anywhere from two days to two months, depending upon the size and experience of the lending institution, the information provided by the buyer and the quality of the buyer. If you are in a short term escrow, this process can be quite maddening.

NOTE: The best way to avoid any frustration is to consult a loan agent and begin the loan qualification process prior to purchasing your home. This is also known as becoming pre-qualified. By becoming pre-qualified you will know how much you can spend on a home and how long it will take to complete the loan process prior to making your initial offer on a home.

Buying a Home with Absolutely No Cash Down!

By Antony Evans

Little-Known Mortgages For Rural Areas Offer Hope to Buyers Who Can't Qualify Elsewhere!

You can buy a new or existing home with no cash down---100% financing and, in some instances, even get your closing costs paid as well.

Here's how to go about it.

1. Contact your city or county Rural Economic and Community Development office (RECDS) and have them send you a copy of the country's maximum loan amounts (they differ from county to county) and a copy of the rural cities and towns on the eligible lending list. Usually, areas of under 25,000 population will qualify for this type of program.

2. Visit and scope out these particular areas to see what housing is available and at what price.

3. Check with builders/contractors who may be constructing new homes in one of the approved rural areas. Tell these builders you have uncovered a new loan program that requires no down payment and 100% financing. Further, enlighten the builder how much easier it would be to sell his/her homes using the no-down payment program.

4. The most important aspect of the Rural Housing Guarantee Loan Program is finding an approved lender close by who finances these types of loans. Contact them for information.

5. Strike up a relationship with a bank or mortgage banker who handles, or would like to finance, your real estate loan. If you locate a bank interest but not on the state-approved list, give them the address of the state office. They can get an approved status in less than three weeks by providing some basic financial information.

No longer do you have to be stymied by that longtime nemesis: "Gee…I just don't have the money to put down on a home." Armed with his Rural Housing Guaranteed Loan Program, you don't need to put down any money. And once you learn more about this particular program, you'll find ways to have most of your (buyer's) closing costs paid in the loan as well.

Basic Information on Rural Housing Loans.

- Buyers must not have owned a home in the last three years.

22

- Buyers must have reasonably good credit for the past 12 months.
- Buyer must be a U.S. Citizen, or have a permanent resident "green card."
- Rural is defined as 10,000 to 25,000 population.
- Home can be new or existing, of any size/maximum one acre.
- If an older residence, the home must be structurally sound, adequate, in good repair and meet energy standard for insulation, etc., It must have adequate plumbing, heating, water, electric, sewer/septic and be free of termites. New homes are exempt from the above except for ground-treated termite control, which is standard in new construction. Your appraiser can furnish this information and sign off.

About the Loan Program

This is a lender loan, not a government loan. Lender uses own forms, just as in any conventional loan. The approved lender completes all the paperwork and funds for the loan.

- Loans may be made up to 100% of appraised value or sales price
- There is no limit on the seller's contribution to buyer's closing costs.
- The borrowers get loans from participating lenders. Loans are then guaranteed by the federal government. Lender gets CRA credit.
- Home must be owner-occupied after purchase.
- Mortgages are 3-years fixed at market rates. No adjustables.
- Maximum loan amount is the same as the HUD maximum for that particular area.
- Loans may include closing costs, guarantee fee, legal fees, title/escrow fees, prepaid items, points, etc.
- There is no PMI (private mortgage insurance) required.
- Repayment ratios can go to 41% MOTL.
- Income limits—115% of median for country.
- Maximum f six persons can live in a three or four bedroom home. All borrowers must be related to, or dependent on, one another.
- Paperwork is minimal. Usually, a Rural Housing Loan can be completed, approved, and funded in less than three weeks.

Narrowing Choices in Buying a Home

By Patrick R. Farrell

Life is full of choices. Life is also busy. It seems that we have more choices now than ever before, but also that we have less time to make decisions. When you're shopping for a new home, probably the largest single investment you'll ever make, this can be a real concern. With all the fine home on the market today, and limited time to look, how do you find the time to make an intelligent, informed decision?

One way is to start with an action plan that will allow you to reduce the number of homes on your shopping list to a realistic number (based on the time you have) and, at the same time, allow you to look at the homes which offer the best possibility of meeting your needs, desires and budget. All you need to get started are the latest real estate listings, a red pen, a few pieces of notebook paper and a pencil with a good eraser.

First, decide what your needs and desires are. Let's look at your needs. What are the most important factors to you in selecting a home? These are the things you are not willing or able to negotiate about. Such a list might look like this: A maximum price of $125,000, three bedrooms, walking distance to the neighborhood school, and off-street RV parking. Give it some thought and make your list.

Next, list your desires. These are the things you want, but they would not be deal-breakers if the home is otherwise perfect. This list might include such things as having at least 2,000 square feet of living space, a mountain view, natural gas heating, and a country kitchen. Only you can draw up a list of your desires. Take some time and write your list.

Why two lists? Because you are going to assign a numerical value to each item on the lists, and the "needs" list is going to be weighted heavier than the "desires" lists. Needs are more important than desires, so they get scores of one to ten points for each. Desires get a score of one to five points each. (If you find a desire that's so important that you want to give it more than five points, move it to the needs list; obviously it's a need to you.)

House Needs/Desires Score Chart

Houses

Needs (score 1 to 10

Price
Bedrooms
Location
RV Parking

Desires (score 1 to 5)

Square Footage
View
Gas Heat
Country Kitchen

Totals

Now take a fresh sheet of paper and your pencil. Down the left side, list your needs and desires. Across the top, write the numbers from one to ten. (This sheet will score ten homes.

Now, start through the listings. When you find a home that seems to meet your basic needs, se the red pen to write a number next to it. That home will be scored in the column under that number. Now, assign values, one to ten for needs, one to five for desires, all the way down the list. Use as many charts as it takes to score all the homes that seem to meet your basic needs.

How do you score a home? Let's look at price as an example. Say your top price is $125,000. A home that is priced at $125,000 would get a score of five. A home priced at $120,000 would get a sic. A home at $115,000 might get a nine or ten. On the other side of the coin, a home priced at $130,000 would get a four. A home priced at $135,000 might get a two or three.

Why bother to list homes that are too expensive? Because sellers often ask more than they really expect to get. Maybe that $130,000 price would come down to $125,000 if you offered it. Or, maybe it wouldn't. Remember that our goal here is to budget you *time*. You may want to include this home because it meets all your other needs and desires, but it is going to get scored down because looking at it may not be the best use of your limited time.

Another Example. Number of bedrooms. Your need is three. Homes that have three would get a score of five points. Homes with four would get a score of seven. Four bedrooms and a den might get a ten. How about two bedrooms and a den? Give it three points. Maybe the den can be used as a bedroom. If it is otherwise acceptable, it may be worth looking at *if you have the time.*

The rest of your needs and desires can be scored in the same way. When you have finished the listings, go back and look at the scores you have given the homes on your charts. At about this point in the process, I usually go back over the list and make some adjustments. Homes that looked pretty good at the beginning may not look so good in light of the later choices. Go ahead and make corrections and changes. This is not a tax return; it's your tool to use as you wish. Feel free to rescore as many homes as you like. (That's why I told you to use a pencil with an eraser for this part.) When you are happy with your list, add up the scores.

The next step is to figure out how many homes you have time to look at. This will depend on you and the size of the area you have to cover. An urban area will allow you to see more in a given time. A rural area will take longer to cover, so fewer homes can be seen. If you think you have time for twelve homes, take the twelve top scores and that's your shopping list. (But keep the list hand; you may have more time than you think.)

Don't try to look at them in the order of the scores you gave them. You'll probably lose too much time driving back and forth. At this point you may choose to contact a real estate professional to help you. Let the professional plan your itinerary and show you the homes you have selected.

Show your chart to your agent or broker. Let him or her see what your needs and desires are, and how you have scored the relative values of each factor. This chart will give him or her a strong understanding of exactly what you are looking for. And your professional may know things about the homes on your list that you don't know. Maybe a price just came down, and that fact may boost an "also ran" to the top of your list.

This system can also be used to evaluate homes as you look at them. Use a fresh chart with the same lists of needs and desires, but this time score the homes as you see each one. The charts become memory aids to help you keep the different homes you look at straight in your mind. (Be sure to use the pencil, you may need to re-score a few homes.)

This system will help you make the best use of your time, and it will help you focus your thoughts on those things that are truly important to you. It will also help you enjoy the experience a little more. You will have the peace of mind of knowing that you're using your time wisely, and that you are looking at the homes with the greatest potential of meeting your needs and desires.

When a *Bad* Location Makes Bargains—and Sense

By Rob DiSilvestre

Location, location, location. How many times have we all heard this real estate mantra? Stay away from busy streets, poor school districts, commercial borders. Real estate agents shun their listings and shield buyers from these areas. "Everyone" knows that a bad location is a sure bet for depressed pricing and difficulty in selling.

Whoa! Depressed price? Tough to sell? Sounds like an opportunity for the savvy buyer and a thorough real estate agent. There is good news about "bad" real estate. First, prices are as much as 20% lower than neighborhood comparables. Sellers are often more flexible when it comes to creative financing proposals. There is plenty of time to carefully evaluate the property before making a purchase officer. You may be able to mitigate the negative aspects of the property, make it work for you and live in a home you otherwise couldn't afford.

This evaluation should first and foremost include an analysis of your specific needs versus the property's negative aspects. For example, how about living on a busy street, say with a bus stop in your front yard? Is the bus stop kept neat? Is there some barrier or landscape shielding the stop from the property? Are you the type of person who would use the bus? Is the structure sufficiently sound-proofed to mitigate the traffic sounds? Assuming you don't—and won't—have small children, you presumably can stay out of the road. Maybe traffic is only bad at rush hour and then only in one direction. You may work a different shift, work at home or commute in traffic.

A busy street in a popular school district is an excellent place for a family with teens to look for a home they couldn't otherwise afford. Without a driver's license, living on a bus line becomes a priority. To a committed bachelor, living next6 to the local tavern parking lot might be nirvana. I once bought a new home next door to the local fire station in a quiet suburb. The extra landscape barrier and $25,000 double garage/workshop the builder gave me, more than compensated for the very occasional late night siren.

Even high crime areas can have their devotees. The Fourteenth Street corridor in Washington, D.C. is about as depressed an area as there is in the nation. Surrounded by drugs, poverty, high crime and a truly bad school system, there is a thriving real estate market. Abandoned, century-old townhouses are being sought by an active homosexual community. Once renovated, the homes are truly magnificent. Sophisticated protection systems address the drug-crime problem. Schools are simply not important. These real estate bargain hunters and pioneers have created some special communities out of what once were simply slums.

A home with power lines in the backyard will afford privacy, space and quiet. A condo in the middle of a busy commercial district will be convenient if you work in the area during the week and peacefully deserted on the weekends. If you work in a city, adding 15 minutes each way to your commute could get you 15 miles farther out of the city than the typical suburb; maybe into the country. Simply try to find a highway that extends beyond an outer suburb.

Once you have decided that the negative aspect of a property is not as important as your specific need, try to identify ways you might alleviate whatever problem the property has. Maybe you can put up some type of landscape barrier around that bus stop. Perhaps some soundproofing can be added to the home on a busy street. Fencing might keep children away from the power lines. Trees, dunes, walls and fences go a long way toward keeping the outside out. Develop an action plan. Estimate the cost of implementing it.

Now you can negotiate a favorable deal on what is hopefully an already depressed price. Of course, once you purchase the property, you will become a potential seller. *Don't despair.* Remember, you bought the place, so there is a market out there for your home. When you want to sell, all the standard rules for interviewing real estate agents apply, with a few extra questions thrown in. Does the agent recognize the steps you have taken to mitigate the "problems" with your property? Is the agent realistic? Don't believe the agent who says your improvements eliminate the problems that got you your bargain in the first place. These problems will be recognized by the next buyer. You are looking for the agent who says that the changes you have made will minimize the difference between the most expensive home in your neighborhood and your home. Consider someone who works primarily with buyers in a price range just under the high end of your neighborhood so that to his/her potential buyers, your home is in a neighborhood they couldn't ordinarily afford.

Set a minimum price for your home, tell your realtor what it is and stick to it. Be patient, and make sure you have a realtor who is, too. And like the seller before you, consider some creative financing alternatives you might be willing to offer. Publicize these offers.

Congratulations. You have successfully purchased, fixed and sold a home in a bad location. On reflection, your home was a bad location in a good area *for you*, which is another way of saying good location.

Which brings us back to the three most important things in real estate.

Location, location, location.

The Master Planned Community

By Gloria Morris

Why should you consider a master planned community when selecting your new home? Some people adore this type of housing, and some can't tolerate the togetherness. However, it's certainly worth your time to investigate this option. Here is a definition and some facts that might help you make your decision.

The master planned community is a development created with mixed use of land for residential, commercial, and recreational purposes, clustered around open areas left in a natural state. Neighborhood streets include cul-de-sac and loop roads which restrict through traffic. Pedestrians have access on walking paths. Heavy use of landscaping and green belts are major design elements, and design guidelines control the exterior appearance of buildings, signs, etc. Some are widely diversified including a spectrum from condos to light industry, and others are designed for a common interest such as adults only.

Sometimes called New Towns or Garden Cities or PUDs (planned unit development), they are communities in which all aspects of development are plotted before building begins. The earliest on record is Miletus in Greece which began in the fourth century B.C. and experiments in housing designed to escape crowded urban centers, and has continued through the centuries. The concept became popular again after Congress passed the 1961 Housing Act permitting the Federal Housing Administration to insure condominium mortgages, giving the tax break of home ownership to apartment dwellers. American prototypes include Reston, Virginia, and Columbia, Maryland, built in the 1960s as new self-sustaining communities based on state-of-the-art urban planning.

Security is the number one reason many buyers give for deciding on a master planned community. Many employ sophisticated closed-circuit television surveillance systems, and most feature gates at the entrances. These gates are often manned by security personnel, and the shared cost makes this luxury affordable.

An example is Las Colinas, a 4,000-acre community in Irving, Texas, which boats a highly sophisticated communications center. The security system is computer controlled and provides immediate aid from police, firemen, and medical professionals.

Another feature you might consider important is the protection of the environment around your home. Parks, greenbelts, bike and jogging trails, and wooded areas can be found in nearly every planned community. The buyer has the assurance they will be preserved and maintained properly, and there won't be any grim surprises later.

For your convenience the PUDs feature shopping, schools, and recreational facilities nearby. Some are planned with specific amenities as a focal point such as: golf, swimming, tennis courts, etc. Equestrian communities, for example, have developed for horseback-riding, polo, etc., in Illinois, Utah and California. Many feature sailing, and other water sports.

Dearborn Park, just south of Chicago's Loop, is a good example of one whose location near the workplace is key. It is within walking distance to work for many of its young, professional residents.

Southbrook, Annandale, Minnesota's newest premier residential community is still under construction. It will feature secluded neighborhoods in the midst of rolling hills, reflecting ponds, and a championship golf course.

If you are considering a short-term situation, the assurance that your home will sell quickly at a good price is comforting. These planned communities hold their value well, and the attractive settings and amenities that attracted you will be selling points for you.

But, what about the down side? Are master-planned communities right for everyone? No, along with the attractive amenities come the necessary adherence to the community concept.

One criticism is that the deed restrictions are often excessive. This is a very important element to research. If you are considering a specific master-planned community, talk with people who live there. Most are thrilled with the socialization that is possible with the health club, golf course, swimming pool, club house for crafts, etc. Team sports usually abound, with leagues for baseball, basketball, softball, swimming and other sports. Civic associations provide all kinds of support groups and programs for adults and children. But you may not care to be this involved with your neighbors.

One of the biggest differences between living in a single-family detached house on a half-acre lot is the reality that high-density living requires residents to conform to rules and regulations. Even though the higher density pushes houses closer together and there's room for a ball field or an Olympic-size pool, some people cannot tolerate this.

If you want the freedom to paint your home any color you choose or to add on according to your own whims, the planned community is not for you. If you would rather not become involved in community activism, that is also an important element to consider. Deed restrictions are meant to safeguard the homeowner's investment, and they are enforced. Generally the facilities are constructed by the developer, and the homeowners' association eventually takes control of maintenance responsibilities. The shared amenities require shared responsibility.

Also, beware of the hard-sell marketing tactics of some PUDs, particularly the "theme" projects that make you think of a Disney movie. You want to be sure that clever marketing isn't covering up inferior construction or substandard planning. You should study the plan carefully in terms of lifestyle, your needs and desires, and not be swayed by a gimmicky sales pitch.

In 1997, The National Association of Home Builders (NAHB) reported, "The zoning concept of the master planned new communities, which emerged in the 1960s and 1970s, gives developers more flexibility in planning their communities to preserve natural features such as streams, valleys and steep slopes, and to reduce costs of extending infrastructure to all portions of site."

The NAHB cited The Woodlands near Houston, Texas, designed in the 1970s, as still evolving. A 30-year plan built by 20 independent builders, it will eventually be developed to include seven villages. The early Woodlands villages have held their value extremely well. In the 1990s the newest Woodlands neighborhood has discarded the loop roads and cul-de-sacs in favor of a more pedestrian-friendly modified-grid street layout, called the traditional design concept. This PUD which stresses "true harmony with nature" offers a forest, ponds and lakes as part of everyday life.

Will you find the perfect environment in a master planned community? Only you can answer that question. Sit down with a pad and pencil and define the features that are important to you and your family. And draw up your own master plan.

Remember, It's Your House

By April Miller

You have just bought the perfect house and moved in. Now you can fix up the bathroom, build a fence, rip out the kitchen wall, add a family room, or even paint your new house. Where do you start? Where do you find a reliable as well as a good contractor? And you need to find a good one. There are too many out there that just don't do the job right the first time.

If you are new to an area, the first thing you should do is look around your neighborhood and watch for building going on. Ask the people who are actually living through construction if they would rehire this particular contractor and why. Or ask where you work to see if anybody has recently remodeled, or if a friend of theirs has remodeled.

Get the telephone number of these people's contractors. In fact, get several numbers, even if you have to get a few from the telephone book. Set up some appointments on the same day. That way you don't have to kill five days waiting around for people to show up. Some contractors don't show up at all or even call to say they are going to miss their appointment. Toss those numbers right away. If they can't show up for an appointment, will they show up for your job on a daily basis?

Make notes about each contractor. Does he come dirty like he just was working? (That can be a good thing.) Does he bring a tape measure and take measurements so he can figure out the amount of material he will use? He should do this if he is serious about taking your job. If you interview more than five, you might get confused about who said what, so write things down.

Before you actually show the contractor what you want, have a list ready. That way you won't forget anything. You might even give a list to each contractor so that he will know how to bid the job. Of course, if you add things as you see each new contractor, the bids will be different.

Always get more than one bid and opinion on your job. Someone may suggest something you never thought of, maybe a different set-up on kitchen cabinets or lighting. Also, ask if the contractor does some of the work himself. Is he on the job every day, or does he send a crew and only check in by phone? I prefer a contractor who is on the job at least part of the day. That way, I can ask him questions and make suggestions. Any problems that come up can be solved right away that day.

Does the contractor clean up at the end of the day or do you have to climb over debris to walk through your own house? Does the contractor keep to his time schedule? Those questions could save you a lot of grief. Our remodel in a second home took over a year because we were only there once a month to see the progress. When we called to tell him we were on our way, he always had five guys there busting their butts as we pulled in the driveway. Maybe I should have called more often and just told him we were on our way.

Once you have hired someone, have a constant list of questions going. The only stupid question is the unasked one. If the answer doesn't seem right, question the contractor again. We had a fire pit built in our backyard. The contractor put a drain in the bottom of the pit so rain wouldn't collect. Great idea, right? I noticed the drain pipe was plastic and questioned him about it. He said, "heat rises and won't affect the pipe at all." The pipe melted the first time we used it, and when it rained, we had a small pond. What were we going to do, rip out the firepit and planter to correct this a year later?

You should insist on having a contract with an agreed upon completion date with a penalty for not finishing on time. We thought the contractor that took a year to remodel our second home would be efficient because he was working for some friends of ours. He did great work, but he had too many projects started at the same time. I finally treated him like a little kid and drove two hours one way every two weeks to check up on him.

An important thing also to do, is to write on walls or leave Post-It notes for the contractor as the construction progresses. Now is the time to add a plug, change the door frame, or reposition a light fixture. In our kitchen, we wanted cable added for the TV, and the phone needed to be moved. I used chalk and wrote on the walls, just like the contractors do, to remind them where the cable and phone should go. If they forget to add something, you either live without it and are mad you didn't say something. Or they have to rip out part of your wall to fix their mistake and hopefully wallpaper wasn't already up. This only adds to the time delay and frustration on everyone's part.

Remember, this is your house. These people work for you. If you really want something, ask for it and wait until you find someone to do the job your way. If you are a woman and are interviewing the contractors, make sure they know you are also a decision maker. My husband only wanted to see results, write the checks, and not be bothered with the contractors. Some men might like to take on the responsibility of hiring the contractor. Fine with me, but if you are the one home and dealing with the contractor, you better like him too.

I've hired six different contractors, two plumbers, two electricians, and four painters. Only one of the contractors will ever work at my house again. The rest either did sloppy work, took too long, or I had to babysit them every single day.

You would think that hiring a painter would be easy. Our perfect painter got carpel tunnel syndrome and had to give up painting. Our interior decorator sent a painter over that didn't tape off anything. He painted all the brand new brass on our new windows along with painting the glass. He claimed that he would just clean up after. It took him three days to not finish two bedrooms. I sent him packing without finishing the job.

The bottom line is, don't let anyone talk you into something you do not want, like, or need. One contractor insisted that I needed a warming oven and talked my husband into it (that's why he stays out of it now). I knew we would never use it. It turned out that the contractor hadn't measured the cabinets correctly, and we didn't have enough for the warming oven after all. Aw, shucks. That saved me the price of the drawer and installation.

Just remember as you are walking through the disaster area that used to be your house, someday this will be the house you dreamed about.

Finding the Right Location for Your New Home

By Marie-Helen Goyetche

Many things should be considered when you're searching for a home. The first is obviously the house itself, but the second (just as important) is the location.

Are you planning to buy a home in the midst of the city's hustle and bustle? Is the sense of a close-knit community in a residential area important to you? Or would you prefer peace and quiet somewhere on a small country road? Your personality will be an important factor when deciding where your next home will be. The location can add to the loving feeling for your new home or it can make you regret your new purchase. To help you decide which location is right, find out what services are important to you, your spouse, and your family. Do you want everything (or almost) to be within walking distance? Do you mind having to take your car? Or do you want to run errands only once a week?

Schools. Are there daycare/nursery schools and elementary schools available in the area for your young children? Are middle and high schools close enough so that the children will not have too long a bus ride? Having the local school right around the corner might not matter if the school doesn't match with your parenting philosophy. Go to the schools, meet the students, the teachers, and the principal. Ask them for their school handbook. Feel free to ask how they deal with important situations such as fighting, racial tension, and religious differences. Do they have extra-curricular activities? Many questions will arise as you make your investigation.

Religious Services: Is your church/synagogue/temple close by? Attend one of their services and talk to those who attended the service. What do they tell you about their parish and the community?

Recreational Centers: Can you find a community center, library, and playground? If your children are older, it might be more important to be near a swimming pool, football field, baseball diamond, or an ice rink.

Health Services: Are there hospitals and/or clinics nearby? Even if you are healthy, accidents will happen. You'll need to know where you can go. Likewise if you own animals, where is the veterinarian?

Stores: Where is the drugstore, convenience store, shopping malls, banks and post office? Will you need to go shopping for one day a week and stock up, or will you be able to get there more often in just a short walk?

Other Things to Consider: Is the house located near a river or lake? If yes, what happens during the spring season? Could your house possibly be in a flood zone? Is the house located near train tracks? If yes, does the train go by after midnight? Are you near a wooded area? If yes, will that be the next site for the big new shopping mall next year? Is the house located near a tourist attraction? If yes, and it's a really big attraction, maybe the house is not suitable, even if it is listed at a very good price.

Are your friends, family, and you going to pay exorbitant long distance charges with the local phone company?

The amount of taxes, school taxes and where the money is spent, can also play an important roles in your decision. Is there a bus service in the area? In the northern states, during the winter months, are the counties putting salt or sand on the roads? How's the snow removal--quick and efficient, or left to be discussed?

You can call the Chamber of Commerce in that county and they'll send you a booklet with all the information about this area. Your realtor can also help you with the prescreening of the area. You can help him/her by determining first, what's on your "must have" list and then on your "would be nice" list.

If you wind up with a few possibilities, get a feel for the area. You can attend local events and meet future neighbors there. Or you can simply knock on a few doors and ask the neighbors yourself. What is it that they especially enjoy or dislike in the community?

There are many important factors involved in order for you and your family to choose the right area and surroundings for everyone involved, before you purchase your new home.

Shopping For a Garage Door and Opener

By Suzan A. Chapman

The following are questions that you should have answers to when you are shopping for a garage door and opener:

Questions for You, the Buyer

1. What size door do you want a price on? These sizes are usually expressed in width and height. The most common sizes are: eight feet, nine feet, 16 feet, and 18 feet wide. These widths are all available in seven or eight feet heights. Example size: sixteen feet wide by seven feet high.

2. What kind of door do you want? Metal doors have taken over the door market. Wood doors still exist, but are not as readily available.

3. Is this to replace an existing sectional door or a one-piece door? If the new door is to replace a sectional door, than this is an "apples-to-apples" application. The one-piece door replacement with a sectional door is an "oranges-to-apples" application. Door companies usually have estimators who can visit the job site. The estimators will be able to inform the customer on what kind of opening preparations may be needed. Sometime sit's just impossible to install a sectional garage door where a one-piece door was.

4. Where are you located? Give the subdivision or the street where the job is located.

Questions to Ask the Seller

1. What gauges do you carry? The gauge of a door is the thickness of the metal used. The higher the number, the thinner the gauge. In the industry, the most common gauges offered are: 36, 25, and 24. Remember, the higher price tag should go with the 24-gauge door.

2. What colors are available? The most popular colors are almond, white and brown.

3. What kind of warranties are available? Some garage doors have a ten-year limited warranty. Others may have a lifetime warranty. Most door companies offer a one-year warranty against defects in workmanship and materials.

4. What options are available? This depends on the door company in your area. Ask if they offer different types of glass other than the standard single-strength glass (SSB). They may surprise you and offer Plexiglas, obscure glass, bronze and decorative glass designs.

Insulation may be available, too. There's no harm in asking if more options exist than the ones I have suggested.

All garage-door openers since 1993 have been designed and manufactured with safety features.

Good quality service is the key to choosing a good garage door opener. Service should be performed on the complete door system. That's the door as well as the opener. These two products need to function as a team. There has been a misconception that once you purchase a garage-door opener the springs are no longer needed. *Not true!* The door has to work well manually before the garage-door opener can be installed.

Every door company has its own way of arriving at prices. A price should include: removing an old door, disposing of the old door, tax, installation and any options. Some companies give a low over-the-counter price and then add for everything else. They may come close to the same all-inclusive price, but the customer is somewhat disenchanted with this approach.

Ideally, most houses are built with attached garages; therefore, we have a tendency to use the garage door like the front entry door. That means parts like springs, cables and gears will wear out quicker on this system.

Keep all of your important papers in a file. When you need service, please be prepared to give a model number when the service person asks. Don't yell "It's your brand and you installed it!"

Have the installer/technician give you a hands-on experience with all the features on your new system. Look at this system as you would a new car; test drive it. Visit the showroom, which is the best place to test out the door or opener's features. The more you familiarize yourself with this system the more you will enjoy owning it; don't be intimidated by the biggest moving appliance in your home.

Water, Water Everywhere

By Susan Clark

It was the first night in our new home. The rain had been falling steadily throughout the day, but it had not dampened our spirits as we fell exhausted into bed. We lay there, quietly discussing how lucky we felt; how fortunate we were to finally be able to have a home of our very own. The soothing sound of raindrops on the roof lulled us into a peaceful state as we drifted off to sleep.

The sudden "gush" of a torrent of rain forced us both out of bed in a flash. "What in the world was that?" I screamed as the sound of roaring water rushed to my ears. Our quiet, lovely home had instantly turned into a roaring river of water-coming from the closet!

Unfortunately, this is a true story. In spite of the fact that we had purchased the services of an independent inspector, our worst fears materialized the very first night in our new home. The roof was bad. The steady rain during the day had accumulated under the shingles and eventually burst through the bad plywood—directly in the middle of the master bedroom closet!

Water is a very powerful and insidious force. It can destroy entire beach front blocks in seconds or take years to wear away at a coastline. It can do the same thing to your home. Unfortunately, many of the signs of water damage are hidden or disguised as other problems. But there are clues that help you spot water damage in your new home.

Ceilings. Ceilings are the obvious place to look for signs of water damage. Brown, circular stains, especially along walls or in the corners are strong evidence that water leaked through that spot at one time. Many homeowners use a waterproof paint to try and disguise damage. But if you look carefully from different places in the room, you can usually see a slight difference in the ceiling color.

While you are looking up, examine the metal support strips of dropped ceilings as well. Many times these strips will show a discoloration or even a slight rusting if they were exposed to water. Ceiling tiles may also show signs of crumbling around the edges if they were exposed to a cycle of being wet and dry several times.

Walls. Walls can show many of the same signs of water damage as can ceilings. If you do find a spot on the ceiling, follow that line down a wall and examine it closely. Run your hand over the wall or look down the wall from a close angle. Is it buckled or warped? If it is, chances are good that water ran behind the wall at some time.

Windows and Doors. Give particular attention to the windows and doors in your new home.

These areas are common places for water to seep in, even over long periods of time, without the homeowner noticing.

Door sweeps not only prevent air from entering or escaping your home, they also are supposed to stop water from becoming an unwelcome guest. Inspect these very carefully, making sure they fit snugly against floor and door frame.

Speaking of door frames, examine all sides of the frame, especially if it is wood. Wooden stoops are very susceptible to moisture and insects. This is one area of your home that should be as moisture free as possible.

Rain can enter your home through windows very easily—even when they are closed! Make sure all sides are properly caulked and that the window hardware is in good working condition. If the window does not close properly, water will defiantly find its way through even the tiniest crack. Scrutinize the sill very carefully. Stained wood will appear slightly washed out if water damage is present. (No pun intended!) It's a bit harder to spot damage to painted wood, but it, too, will have a tell-tale discoloration. Also, push on several spots along the sill with your thumb. Does the wood "give" at all? If it does, water damage could be the culprit.

No one can inspect thoroughly enough to absolutely guarantee that your new home is free of water damage. But if you look in most of the obvious places, you can feel assured you have done the best you can in preventing future headaches. Just remember, though, that no one messes with Mother Nature, so just make sure you are as informed as possible when selecting your new home!

Buyer Beware

By Joy Duffy

When purchasing a property, you may run into costly problems like: unclear titles, easement problems, code violations, structural damage, zoning, faulty sea walls, leaking roofs, termites, cracked pools, and water-seeking tree roots. You need to understand the possible problems you could encounter in order to make an informed choice when buying a property, so that you can guard against these problems with clauses in your contract, including a provision stating who pays for needed repairs.

Almost all contracts call for the seller to pass clear title and require the property be unencumbered by liens. Your contract should also call for a survey that shows encroachments, like the neighbor's shed or fence. If your contract doesn't offer this protection, ask for it in an addendum. A survey will show easements that allow electric or telephone companies access to your property to repair their lines. There may be a right-of-way easement for a common driveway between you and your neighbor. Beware of such an easement, especially if you intend to lease the property. Some communities have easements behind houses for garbage collection. Sure, it's pleasant not to have to ride down the street and see garbage in front of the house. But there is a drawback; you cannot fence your entire property. Different parts of the country have different easements. The west has water easements between anchors. Florida has air and mineral rights. All such rights may be reserved by former owners. If a former owner reserves these rights, it may cost thousands to clear them, but you must clear them or someone may come on your property to drill for oil. Most urban banks will not finance properties unless all rights are transferred to the buyer.

Also, beware of bad roofs and termites. Make your contract subject to a roof and termite inspection, especially if buying as is. Never believe the seller-always check yourself.

A wide spectrum of problems comes under the heading of code violations. If a seller builds another room without a permit, it's a code violation. Permits are also needed for fences, driveways, pools, wells, sheds, and other things. In this age of computers everything about every property is recorded somewhere so don't try to beat these guys. When purchasing, check with the city to be sure the seller did everything according to code, especially if there is an addition or closed-in garage or carport.

Here is an example that covers both code violations and easement rights. It shows how expensive violations can become. Hollywood, Florida, reserves an easement called swale rights. Barry bought a house he loved. When he first looked at the house he noticed that there wasn't enough room to park in front of the house. He didn't care because he noticed three tiny trees in the swale. He figured he would remove one and park there. Wrong! That tree belonged to the city. Barry didn't know that so he dug up the tree. Code enforcement patrol came around and gave him a citation for destroying city property. They gave him 20 days to replant a black olive tree of comparable size or they would fine him $150 a day until he did. It was the fourth of July and Barry was having a picnic. All his friends teased him and said things like, "Are you going to let the city tell you what you can do on your own property?" After a few beers, Barry decided to ignore the citation. He tore it up and burned it in the barbecue grill amid cheers from his friends. When he sold the property, he went to the attorney's office expecting a check for $17,000. Instead, he found a closing statement showing he owed $23,000 more than the sale price. The closing statement revealed a lien for a $40,500 tree. After a month of negotiation with the city, he closed the deal, but Barry lost his profit and still had to replant the tree.

Janice bought a property with a closed-in carport. The day after the sale closed, here comes code enforcement. They made her rip out the walls because they were put in without a permit. This foolishness can not only get expensive to correct, but can also devalue the property. An extra room or bath can add as much as $10,000 to the price of a home. If you get caught without a permit and have to tear it out, there goes ten grand.

Code enforcement people ride the streets every day, including holidays, looking for sneaky people trying to do things behind their back. Do not take the chance.

Structural problems are costly to repair. Houses get horizontal settlement cracks with time—this is normal. However, large vertical cracks are not. If you see vertical cracks, especially around rooms that have been added, beware. Andrew noticed such a crack and pointed it out to his realtor. She warned him against the house, but he loved it and insisted on buying it. Thankfully, the realtor put in a clause stating that the buyer must approve a structural inspection. The report showed that the room, added with a permit, was built over unstable sand that was shifting because of nearby blasting. In order to fix the problem, cement would have to be force-pumped under the entire foundation. The cost to repair, $50,000.

Zoning is another potential problem. Just because you see a house in an area full of duplexes, that doesn't mean you can change the house into two units. If you expect to change any property into rental property, go to city zoning department and make sure you are allowed to expand. Get it in writing. If a duplex you are considering looks altered, check it out.

Vacant houses can be trouble. Some houses are vacant because the building is substandard or obsolete. These problems can be corrected if you are willing to foot the expense. However, the unscrupulous owners know the property has major problems and decide to cover them up. Decayed and rotten wood can be covered up with sheetrock, putty and paint. A leaky roof can be patched long enough to sell. A faulty septic tank won't show if no one uses it. Houses that have been vacant for long periods may be eaten by termites. They eat the wood from the inside out so the damage doesn't show until it's too late. If the house was previously rented and is now vacant, maybe the tenants did something insidious because they were angry with the landlord. Tenants sometimes do vindictive things, like pouring cement down the toilet. Have the utilities turned on and check the house out thoroughly.

Beware of seawalls: they are extremely expensive to fix. Get an inspection even if the seawall looks okay. Never attempt to fix one yourself unless you are an expert. A faulty seawall can undermine your house as well as the neighbors' and drag you into a lawsuit.

A leaky pool can be easily hidden by an unscrupulous seller. Losing water and having to refill the pool wouldn't be so bad. But where is that leaking water going? It's undermining the house, of course.

Beware of trees with wandering roots. Those roots are seeking water and will find it in the ground, the lake, or your pool. Roots grow through cracks in seawall, foundations, driveways, sidewalks, and even septic tanks. They are like ravenous little monsters wreaking havoc on everything they encounter. If you see big trees, look for damage. They may have to be removed before they damage your or your neighbors' property.

Paint: The Beautiful Cover-Up

By Bradford H.Caffey

"A little spackle, a little paint, can make your dream home what it ain't."

What's underneath that last coat of paint? Do you know when paint becomes the great cover-up? How can I know when the home, in which I'm investing the majority of my monthly earnings, is a solid and secure investment?

These questions run through the mind of every homeowner whenever s/he buys a home. Experience sometimes teaches us a hard, expensive lesson whenever we avoid asking the right questions or fail to probe beneath the surface of the painted walls, around windows, over baseboards and beside door casings.

One homeowner in Louisville, Kentucky, bought a home which had been advertised as a "Premium Quality Home in a Prestigious Neighborhood." The man soon discovered huge, one-half inch cracks above the baseboard in the living room. The cracks had been expertly filled with caulk, and after the paint had dried, the cracks were hidden beautifully. The man discovered other irregularities besides a door casing in the dining room. The filled cracks prompted him to examine the rest of the house where he discovered other flaws above the baseboard and beside door and window casings.

Fortunately for this new homeowner, the reality firm with whom he dealt insisted that the previous owner pay to have the repairs done professionally. New drywall was added and the rooms repainted. In this case, the shoddy workmanship in a quality home was inexpensively correctable.

Considering how easily cracks, holes and blemishes can be hidden with spackle, caulk or paint, the prospective buyer should poke and probe into every nook and cranny of the house before signing a contract. Certainly a small bead of caulk around door, windows and at the top of baseboards, or crown molding, makes the paint job nearly perfect.

However, the home buyer's concern about caulk and paint cover-up occurs when large cracks along the edges of the woodwork are hidden by the painted caulk. What caused these cracks? Did the foundation shift enough to pull the walls away from the wood e3dge? If so, the homeowner needs to be aware of a potentially expensive structural problem rather than a simple drywall replacement. If the large cracks are a result of shoddy workmanship, other areas of the house exhibit the same lack of attention to detail as the existing caulk-filled crack? It's the attention to detail which yields success in any profession. Certainly this would be true in the building profession as well.

Another paint cover-up occurs inside or outside the house whenever loose or chipping paint is painted over without proper surface preparation. These cover-ups are readily visible, and look like blisters underneath the new coat of paints. One can take his thumb or fingernail and scrape these blister-like areas, and the paint will scrape off easily. A word of caution about using a thumb or fingernail to scrape the paint: the dried paint underneath the new coat of paint can easily penetrate the cuticle underneath your nail and cut like a knife.

Sometimes we find paint flaws where the blistered paint is removed to the bare wood and a coat of paint is added without removing the layers of paint surrounding the blistered area. When this cover-up is completed, an unsightly depression occurs. This paint cover-up is more prevalent than the painted blister effect mentioned earlier. We find these divot-like depressions in older homes, and usually the flaws are caused by painters who have not sanded the wood smooth all around the divot before applying the next coat of paint.

Of course, the painted wood surface can be redone by sanding away the excessive layers of paint until the board is free of the extra layers. Then the prepared surfaces can be repainted with one or two even coats of paint on the surface. Remember however, restoring surfaces in this fashion is hard work and takes a great deal of time.

Yet, when looking at a house where some of the window casing or the wood trim has the noticeable depressions in the painted surfaces, you could offer the owner less money and do the sanding and painting yourself. Or, you could tell the owner to have the paint flaws fixed before you would be interested in purchasing the house. If you plan to sand and paint the marred surfaces, try to determine the number of hours it will take you to complete the job. Then decide how much money you wish to make per hour sanding and stripping the old paint away. Deduct that amount from the lowest price which the owner will take for the house, and tell the owner why and how you derived at this figure.

Although the next condition of painted surfaces does not consist of a cover-up, it could be the most crucial paint blunder, the prospective home buyer faces. It's the ugly paint splotches on the brick around exterior windows, door, fascia boards and down-spouts. Would you buy a house where the brick surfaces around the above mentioned areas and has paint slopped or dropped on the brick?

Yes, you can remove the paint with a wire brush and a mild acid or by having sad blasting done. However, in the author's experience, the brick always appears lighter where the paint has been removed. Your best bet is to find another home to buy and avoid the added hassle of paint on the brick around exterior wood surfaces unless, of course, you simply do not mine the way it looks.

Even though paint, spackle and caulk add beauty and a touch of professionalism to painted surfaces, the home buyer would be well advised to guard against their over-use. When used to conceal flaws, damaged areas or inferior products and workmanship, these two items make out like masked bandits.

The Engineering Report

By Crhistopher Lukas

So you've found this lovely house, just the home or investment property you've been searching for. You've put up a small amount of money for the binder and have begun to look for a mortgage. Meanwhile, being prudent, you take another look around the premises: You go through the basement, actually get a ladder and climb up to look at the roof. You check out the circuit-breakers (making sure there's enough power), and examine the exterior paint job for wear-and-tear. Satisfied that your practiced eye has done a good job, you have no qualms about signing a contract when your lawyer draws it up.

A few days after that, a friend asks, "Did you get an engineering report of a professional home inspection service?"

"Don't need one," you reply. "I checked things out myself."

It is indeed a popular, "money-saving" idea that some home buyers and investors have these days to skip a professional engineering look-over. Many feel that the experience of buying their last house, or the apparent good shape of this new one, means they don't need to bother. This can be a foolish, and sometimes disastrous mistake, especially considering that an engineering (or "home inspection") report can cost as little as $400, and seldom more than $750, including an examination for termites.

Those few bucks may save thousands of dollars and many nights of worry later. Here's why.

Peace of Mind. Let's assume you're relatively experienced. Your examination of that pleasant house (say, it was built in the late 1940s and located in a good area of a modest suburb) satisfied you at the time. But, one night *after* signing the contract, you realize that you forgot a few things: You didn't take a plate off one of the light switches to see what kind of insulation the house contains. You didn't look at the mortar between the bricks in the chimney. As a matter of fact, you didn't even check to see how old the furnace and water heater were.

Then, you remember the clause in the contract which goes something like:

Purchasers have inspected the premises and agree to accept same as "AS IS" condition, reasonable wear and tear excepted, the Sellers having made no representation in connection therewith.

Now you start wondering, did you miss something crucial? How about the garage; you didn't even look there. What condition was it in? And the pipes. You forgot to see what they were made of—copper or iron.

In fact, it is unlikely that you—or any buyer—will remember all the things to check for. And why should you? That's not the business you're in. These are things an experienced engineer might notice that a buyer—even a long-time buyer—might never see. Unfortunately, it's too late to hire an engineer. You've signed the contract.

Professional Expertise. Plunking down a few hundred dollars for a professional inspection is a cheap way of obtaining peace of mind. And, obviously, it should be done *before* signing a contract, just as any *binder* you sign should state that the sale *is contingent* on a satisfactory inspection by a trained professional.

What is meant by a "trained professional?" Not all inspectors are structural engineers, so you need to ask about credentials. A "Home Inspection" service company should be requested to give the qualifications of whoever is going to do your inspection, because an *engineer* will be able to check out the following areas of a home with special expertise.

Exterior:

- Siding—what it's made of, how old it is, what condition it's in.
- Foundation—what's it made of, whether there are any cracks.
- Roof—the age, composition, and condition of the roofing materials.
- Chimney(s)—what areas and functions they serve, the construction, the condition, and recommended repairs (if any).
- The fascia, soffits, and eaves—looking for potential mildew or rotting
- Screens and storm windows
- Gutters and leaders
- Porches and decks
- Walkways—cracks or potential damage in the cement
- Walls or fences around the property
- Drainage and grading of the property—does rainwater flow *toward* or *away from* the basement walls?
- Driveways
- The garage and other structures

○ Swimming pool (if any)

Interior:

○ Kitchen—how old are the appliances; do they work? Is three point electrical grounding available? Does the plumbing work, or are there leaks? What's the condition of the linoleum floor?

○ Bathrooms—are the fixtures adequate and in good shape? What's their life expectancy?

○ Stairs—are they safe?

○ Walls and ceilings—what state is the plaster in? Do walls show normal or abnormal settling?

○ Windows and doors—are there broken windows? Do they open and close easily? Should they be replaced with double-glazing?

○ Fireplaces

○ Smoke detectors

○ Attic—access, insulation, ventilation

○ Insulation

Basement, crawl spaces:

Are they finished or raw?

○ Is there evidence of water penetration, degradation of mortar?

○ Is there a sump pump?

Heating and cooling systems:

○ Age and condition of systems

○ Presence of asbestos

○ Proper shut-off valves and switches

Plumbing and electrical systems:

- Specifications, power, condition, adequacy

This listing is a fairly typical one for most inspections conducted in our particular community—a suburb of New York City. Some engineers will report in greater detail on one or more areas of the home.

A Back Door. While the home inspection company does not *guarantee** any of the building's elements (except for the absence of termites), their report can serve to alert you to a vast array of conditions—good and bad—*before* purchase. In other words, while the engineering report itself is not a legal document, it does provide a legal way for a prospective buyer to change his or her mind, even after signing that binder and putting up a fee to hold the house. Here's how that works.

Let's assume that when you signed your binder, you did make sure to include a phrase that permitted you to withdraw your bid if you didn't get a satisfactory engineering report. (Usually, you are required to have this done within ten days of signing the binder, which gives you plenty of time.).

If your report actually uncovers something which causes you deep concern, you have time to check it out in detail, or you may simply tell the real estate broker or your lawyer that the engineering report is *not* satisfactory, and that you want to withdraw your offer to buy. At that point, the binder becomes null and void.

Isn't it worth four or five hundred dollars to protect yourself against the possibility of buying a house for—say $250,000—which might, later, turn out to be a lemon, with problems that could cost thousands of dollars to remedy?

A check-over by an engineer, or at the very least, a qualified home inspector, is the best answer to your night-time peace of mind and the security you deserve when you're buying a house.

*Generally, the inspection will contain a phrase such as the following: "This report reflects our professional opinion of the property as of the date of this inspection...we do *not* make any warranty as to the property's future condition."

Help! It Doesn't Fit Through the Door!
Twenty Tips for Purchasing Large-Ticket Items
By Eileen J. Safran

Your glistening new refrigerator sparkled like the morning sun. There was just one "little" problem. The existing refrigerator space did not allow sufficient room for the door of the new unit to open freely. You measure incorrectly and you cannot return the unit.

It was love at first sight between you and your new sofa. Delivery day finally arrived and you were devastated when the couch would not fit through the front door. Yes, you had ascertained that your empty living room wall would accommodate this particular sofa. But you had never considered the width of the doorway in relation to the size of the new furniture.

These situations occur every day in the purchasing world of "large ticket items." Remember, if you buy something that does not fit, you may have no recourse.

Review the following tips prior to purchasing an appliance or piece of furniture. Careful reading should result in a successful transaction and an everlasting love affair between you and your new decor.

1. Determine your budget. Identify your specific needs. Set priorities and stick to them.

2. Research before you buy. Appliances are reviewed in publications such as "Consumer Reports." Such magazines describe the pros and cons of a specific model.

3. Carefully measure the space to be occupied by the new addition. Remember to measure entrance doorways as well as interior doorways. Did you know that a king size bed may easily pass through a particular door because it usually arrives in two pieces, but a queen size bed which arrives in one piece may not squeeze through the same entrance!

4. Read all energy labels before buying. The purchase price of a self-defrosting refrigerator may fall within your budget, but the effect on your electric bill may be staggering.

5. Review operating and maintenance instructions. Is that fabric stain resistant? Is your electrical system sufficient to carry that particular air conditioner? Find out before you buy!

6. Check prospective furniture for quality in workmanship. Rough edges, sticking drawers, patches of dried glue are all signs of poor workmanship. A clue to the quality of goods can often be found in hidden areas where the lazier craftsman tends to be sloppy.

7. Check upholstered furniture for matching patterns. There should be no loose threads or running

colors.

8. Test the furniture. Make certain that it fits your body and your lifestyle. Is it safe? Sit in chairs. Do they wobble? Try all doors and drawers. They should open and close easily.

9. Get your best price! All large-ticket items leave the factory with a tremendous mark-up. Shop around carefully and watch for sales. Keep in mind that January, February, June and August are known for furniture sales.

10. Exercise caution and good judgment when comparison-shopping. Read small print of all ads. Some contain restrictions. Be wary of "bait and switch" tactics. This occurs when an item advertised at a price too good to be true is out of stock. A salesperson then tries to sell you a more expensive item.

11. Always buy from a reputable dealer. Forget "roadside stands." If problems arise at a later date, these dealers may have disappeared.

12. Do not be forced into signing a contract of sale. Remember, once you sign on the dotted line, it is virtually impossible to cancel the order.

13. Know the rules pertaining to layaway sales. You must be made aware of the total cost of the item. This includes tax, delivery and any finance charges. You must also be made aware of the duration of the plan and required payment schedule. Also note whether refunds are available prior to final payment.

14. Understand the warranty. Does it cover parts and labor or just parts? Must you ship the item to the manufacturer or are you covered for the cost of a serviceman visiting your home? Who is responsible for shipping charges if an item must be returned to the manufacturer? Should you keep the original carton? Know the answers to these questions.

15. Be aware of any required maintenance prior to making a purchase. Special care, required for certain items, can become quite costly.

16. Make sure that your sales contract describes exactly what you are purchasing. The brand, color and model number should be clearly stated on your invoice. The quoted sales price should appear for your records.

17. You are entitled to a specific delivery date. Some local governments require that delivery be made within 30 days of the date of sale. If a company wishes to change a delivery date, you are entitled to receive at least one day's notice.

18. Inspect furniture or appliances immediately upon delivery. Do not accept them if there appears to be damages.

19. Keep all documents pertaining to the transaction. These papers include sales receipts, warranties, and care and maintenance instructions. Keep all paperwork in a safe place.

20. Report all problems to your local office of Consumer Affairs.

Just the Facts, Ma'am

By Michael S. Ezell

Finding out about crime in your new neighborhood.

Let's face it, in today's world, crime is a factor in nearly everything. You see it every night on the news, some fantastic account of a bank robbery, shooting, assault, or some other crime that seems to catch the media's eye. The next day, you talk about these stories around the water cooler. Everyone grumbles about the "crazy world we live in these days."

But once the news is over, most people forget about the stories and continue to walk around in what police-officer-safety instructors call "Condition White." That is, oblivious to their surroundings.

This seems to be especially true when people are shopping for new homes. Caught up in the excitement of looking for a new place to live, or perhaps buying that all-important first home, buyers tend to overlook the importance of finding out what kind of neighborhood they are moving into.

That may sound like a pessimistic view of the world; but remember, ultimately you, and not the real estate agent, will be living and raising a family in the neighborhood you choose.

Maybe some people neglect to research this important subject because they just do not know where to start. In reality, this is probably one of the simplest things you will do when buying a new home. It does not cost you anything, and should not take more than an hour or two of your time.

Most police departments divide the cities they serve into what they call "Reporting Districts." This makes it easy to keep track of certain statistics and identify problem areas in the city. The first step for the buyer is to pay a visit to City Hall and find out what Reporting District that fabulous new home is situated in. Just give the clerk the address for the home.

Crime statistic reports are generally compiled on a quarterly basis and sent to City Hall so the mayor and City Council can review the activities of the police department. After being reviewed, this information is available to the public upon request. Ask to see the statistics for burglaries, robberies, etc. in the Reporting District where you are looking to buy. Compare that information to statistics from other areas in which you may be considering purchasing a home.

One other helpful area that people seem to be completely in the dark about is *average response time. Average response time* means the time it takes officers to reach a home after they are dispatched to the call. The area you want to look into is what is usually known as "Priority One Calls" or something similar. These calls are burglaries, robberies, assaults, etc. that are "in progress." Prowler calls and 911 calls that are cut off before the dispatcher can speak to the caller are also Priority One's for my department.

The department I work for keeps statistics in this area the same as they keep track of crimes in the different reporting districts. This information should be available in the same report that contains the number of crimes in your area.

Generally speaking, two to three minutes is a good response time for calls of this type. Sometimes there is an officer right around the corner when the call comes in. Sometimes the officer is across town. The average of these responses for a quarterly period should give you a good idea about the area you are interested in.

If you notice a trend towards high response times for "in progress" crimes, this could mean the area you are considering is extremely busy and usually has a high number of what officers refer to as "hot calls." Although it may appear peaceful and quaint when you drive through with the realtor, high response times for in progress calls may indicate that the neighborhood is quite different when the sun goes down.

There are several other things you can do that will reveal facts about your future neighborhood that dry statistics on paper cannot tell you.

The real estate agent usually works on a schedule that takes prospective buyers into a neighborhood when all the kids are in school and everyone else is at work. Once you find a home you like, go back into the neighborhood at odd times during the day. If you have children try to see whether the kids in the area are around the same age as your own. Look at the foot and vehicle traffic that goes through the area.

If your potential new home is somewhat off the beaten path, but still has an unusually high amount of foot traffic or vehicles traveling through at odd hours of the day or night, this could be indicative of a flourishing drug trade in the area. Again, something unpleasant to think about, but even more unpleasant to discover after you have made what will probably be the largest investment of your life.

Drive around the surrounding areas and look at the neighborhoods. Is there a lot of gang graffiti? Is there an inordinate number of kids running around on the streets during school hours? These things should be taken into consideration. Do all the kids cut through your neighborhood after school? Is the street a local shortcut when traffic is heavy on the main thoroughfares? Burglars thrive in areas where it is not unusual to see strangers walking around, or driving through.

While looking at the different faces your prospective neighborhood wears throughout the day, you may want to take note of how many times you see a marked patrol car drive through the area. Does there seem to be a good high-profile police presence in the area? Are they just patrolling, or do the officers always seem to be in the neighborhood on business?

Although it makes some people nervous wrecks, getting pulled over by the police while you are checking out your new neighborhood may be a good sign. It means they know most of the people or vehicles that belong in the neighborhood and you made them suspicious by driving around apparently without a purpose in the area.

It may seem like an insult that the local police would mistake you for a burglar casing homes, but look at it from the viewpoint of a resident of the area. Would you want the police to investigate someone cruising up and down your street looking at all the homes? Of course you would.

If you do locate officers routinely patrolling the area, flag down a patrol car and ask the officers directly if they have any problems in the area. You may find the local beat officer your most reliable source of information when it comes to finding out about the usual goings-on in your possible new neighborhood.

Once you have decided that the neighborhood is right for you, a source of good information for "crime-proofing" your new home is the police department's Crime Prevention unit. The officers and civilians in this unit are always happy to give out tips on not falling victim to criminals in your area. (Like not allowing bushes to grow tall enough to screen your windows. Bad guys love this!)

Some departments even have personnel in Crime Prevention who will come out and look at your home and offer tips on how to set up good home security. This way, you know the information is based on experience, and not hype put out by alarm-system salesmen or someone trying to sell you security bars for your windows.

No matter which course you decide to take, remember one thing: This is *your* home. You are paying a good chunk of your income for this place and you will be raising your children there. The real estate agent will do everything in his/her power to find you a home that you like, but ultimately, the responsibility for deciding if the home is right for you is yours alone.

Enjoy what may be one of the great moments of your life. Just be sure to step back and look at the big picture. Do not be dazzled by the fantasy white picket fence around your new home and miss the graffiti on the fence around the corner.

How to Find a Friend in Real Estate

By Terri DeGezelle

Picking a realtor to work with in buying a new home or selling your present home can be as important as selecting your obstetrician or your financial advisor. This person will be instrumental in your making the purchase of a lifetime.

Here are a few hints and suggestions you can use when looking for a realtor.

Interview several realtors. Select realtors representing different agencies. In doing so, you'll be able to get a feeling for how personalities differ, as well as how different offices operate and what services they offer. During the interview, you should be able to ask questions and have them answered to your satisfaction. After spending time with these various realtors, you will be able to get a feeling for whom you are most comfortable with.

Here are some questions you'll want to ask:

- Is the person working full-time or part-time in the real estate business. Many people are part-time. Will that fit your needs?

- What is their availability? Are they on a constant on-call status? Will they be available to show your home, handle problems that may arise in the closing, or speak with the other agents that show your home. Do they carry a pager, have voice mail, or have a secretary to get messages to them when they are out of the office?

- What does the agent's firm offer in the line of services to sell your home? Do they offer a free MVA (Market Value Analysis) of your home and property? This service will inform you what the market is like, comparing homes in the neighborhood, same price range and house style. All this information can be discussed and thought through to help with the pricing and realistic expectations.

- Are they involved with the MLS (Multiple Listing Service)? Information about your home will appear with all the other homes for sale in the area. Other real estate companies that are members of the MLS will have information on your home to show their clients.

- Do they offer a walk-through preview of your home to other real estate offices? By walking through, other agents can get a first-hand feeling of your home and pass the informa-tion on to their clients who may be looking for a home just like yours.

Assessing Your Choices. After interviewing, it's important to make some determinations and assessments. With whom did you feel most comfortable? Who could best answer your questions in layman's terms? Who did you feel was most honest, not telling you just what you wanted to hear?

It's important not to pick the realtor who comes in with the highest list price for your home. The price may be over-inflated and then you'll have your home on the market for an extended period of time.

Other Issues. Another important issue to remember is that realtors will always want to have a signed agreement with you. This is important for both of you. This agreement will spell out exactly what is expected of both parties. This way, you both go into a business partnership knowing what is expected of whom.

It's important that a realtor has the communication skills it takes to point our areas in the home that may need improving or repair to bring a quick sale. This communication skill requires a tactful manner and yet an honest approach.

In the end, you are looking for that special someone who has the same goals in mind as you, the seller: a fair market-value price for your home, an early sale, the fewest inconveniences, and the greatest monetary return for you.

Referrals can be a great help; just remember that these referrals should not come from a relative or friend of the realtor.

Making Your Choice. When you have made your decision, the task that lies before you is to have the professional courtesy to let those whom you didn't select know your decision. This is not always fun or an easy matter, but it is necessary. Be honest. One agent may have been full-time versus part-time. One spouse may have felt more comfortable with one agent than another. Whatever the reason, you need to call or drop a note to the realtors you didn't select. Those who don't hear from you will either call or drive by and see a sign. You may find that writing a note is easier than a phone call. The contents of your letter could read as the follows: "After careful consideration we have decided to go with_____in the matter of selling our home. Thank you for your time and effort in this matter." In doing so, you have given the realtor the respect and his/her time the value that is deserved.

For Your Protection

Inspections, fire and hazard insurance, disclosures, and more—some protections that are available to you when buying real estate.

Inspecting Your Investment

The real estate industry has been on the forefront of consumer protection. For instance, many new homes are now covered by HOW (Home Owners Warranty), an insurance program established by the National Association of Home Builders to protect new home buyers against construction defects for ten years after purchase.

Fire and Hazard Insurance

Most lenders require a home buyer to provide at settlement a one-year paid receipt for a fire and hazard insurance policy, often called home owner's insurance. The minimum coverage must equal the mortgage amount. These policies are available from several leading insurance companies throughout your area. Fire and hazard insurance provides protection for fire and other perils to your home and its contents.

Full Disclosure

Real estate law now makes it incumbent upon the seller to tell the buyer of any defects they know of, which would not be apparent in a routine inspection, or be liable for appropriate restitution, thereby providing the buyer with additional protection.

What to Expect from a Home Inspector

What can home buyers expect from a home inspector--besides a bill for $125-$250 (depending on size of property and/or complexity of the inspector's report)?

First of all, expect proof of membership in the American Society of Home Inspectors. Next, expect a quickly-delivered (one- or two-day) written report.

Expect practical returns. While you can see for yourself many flaws in a house, the practiced eye of a professional inspector can probably spot more, especially in areas not easily accessible to a home buyer. Specific information could even reduce the price of a house if the seller will agree the price has not already been discounted for defects.

Possible Repairs

- Serious problems (heating, roofing, plumbing).
- Medium problems (insulation, paint).
- Minor problems (electrical outlets, kitchen sink).

If no serious problems are found, inspection can pay off indirectly in assurance that you are making a sound investment.

Walk-Through Inspection

The purpose of the walk-through inspection several days prior to settlement is to determine if all conditions in the contract are satisfied. The time for the buyer to inspect and note defects for correction by the seller, is during the contract negotiations and prior to signing the sales agreement. Repair or replacement items should be noted in the contract or contingent on a house inspection. Otherwise most resale homes are sold in "as is" condition.

It is up to the buyer to perform the walk-through inspection, not the seller, who may or may not be present. The buyer should be accompanied by the selling agent and the listing agent. The home seller should be sure utilities are on so that equipment can be operated.

Room by Room

The buyer should try all lights and switches; turn all faucets on and off; run the shower; flush toilets; turn on the furnace and central air conditioning (in the off-season, buyer should hire a professional to certify proper functioning of both heating and air conditioning); test all stove burners; test oven at bake and broil; run some ice cubes through disposal to test blades; run dishwasher, washer and dryer through complete cycle; open and close all windows and doors. In short, try everything--even keys and fireplace flue.

All deficiencies should be noted, and funds may be withheld from the home seller by the settlement attorney for repairs, if seller does not correct problems prior to settlement. The selling broker will coordinate with the listing broker and seller to make repairs before settlement, if possible. Upon receipt of bills and notification that repairs are complete, the attorney will release balance of funds to the seller, if money is escrowed for needed repairs.

Inspection Clause

If the buyer chooses to have an inspection, this clause should be included in the purchase agreement or as an addendum. This offer is subject to an inspection by a private inspector of buyer's choice at buyer's expense. Said inspection must be done within five business days of acceptance of this offer. In the event buyer, at buyer's sole discretion, is not completely satisfied, seller hereby agrees that buyer shall have the right to terminate this agreement and to have the earnest monies paid herein returned forthwith. If buyer decides to exercise this option to terminate this agreement, buyer shall do so by serving written notice thereof to seller or seller's agent in person or by registered or certified mail on or before the expiration of said five business day period, where upon all earnest money herein paid shall be returned forthwith to buyer. If said five day period should expire without notice of buyer's intention to terminate this agreement, then this agreement shall be considered in full force and all parts shall be binding.

Fax Agreement

Buyers and sellers usually agree that a facsimile transmission of any original document shall have the same effect as an original. Any signature required on an original shall be complete when a facsimile copy has been signed. The parties should then agree that signed facsimile copies of documents shall be appended to the originals thereof, integrated therewith and give full effect, as if an original.

Adjustable Rate Mortgage vs. Fixed Rate Mortgage

Adjustable Rate Mortgage:

- Initial rate traditionally lower than fixed
- As costs of funds decrease...payment can also decrease.
- Caps control interest rate and payment increase.
- Because the initial interest rate is lower, qualifying income level is lower in some cases.
- Can enable buyer to purchase "more house" for the mortgage amount than a higher fixed rate.
- Provides opportunity to save thousands in interest over period of loan.
- Excellent mortgage program for homeowner planning to move within three to five years.
- Provides opportunity to dramatically reduce monthly payment by paying off a portion of the principal in advance. This payment reduction is not available on fixed rate mortgages.
- As cost of funds increase, monthly payment can increase.
- Buyer shares the risk with the mortgage banker.
- No guarantee of monthly payment over long term.
- Monthly payment can increase to the limit of the caps, if the economy takes a downturn.
- If buyer has stalled earning power, the uncertainty of the monthly payment can be unsettling.

Fixed Rate Mortgage:

- Monthly principal and interest payment remains constant for term of the mortgage
- Buyer has no risk of payment charge.
- Even in the worst economic times, principle and interest payment is unaffected.
- Offers peace of mind and security.
- Offered in a variety of term periods.
- Usually a higher initial rate than ARM at time of loan origination.
- In order to take advantage of lower rates at a later time, the owner must refinance and may have to pay all associated costs of a new mortgage.

Transfer of Equity

There are only three methods with which you may transfer the equity in your present home to another home.

I.   You may go out and buy the home of your choice, contingent upon the sale of your present home. This is commonly called: "Buy High, Sell Low" method.

Advantages:

1. Minimal.

Disadvantages:

1. You must buy high because a contingent offer is worthless to a seller. His/her home is not really sold.

2. You must then try to sell your home quickly, probably at a lower price than if you were under no pressure.

3. Someone else could make an offer on the home you wish to buy, and if you could not remove the contingency, then they would be able to purchase the home.

II. You can purchase the home of your choice on a "straight" offer (no contingencies), and then try to sell your home as quickly as possible. This is called the "Buy Low, Sell Low" method.

Advantages:

1. You do not need to offer more on the home of your choice, since you are not making a contingent offer.

Disadvantages:

1. You are still under pressure to sell your home as quickly as possible, and probably settling for less money in the long run.

2. You run the risk of owning two homes at the same time.

III. You can put your present home on the market, and sell it "subject to the purchase of the home of your choice." This is called the "Buy Low, Sell High" method.

Advantages:

1. You can wait for the best offer on your present home. You are under no pressure to sell.

2. You can then go out and purchase the home of your choice at the best price.

3. When purchasing the home of your choice, you know exactly how much equity you have available for down payment, etc..

Disadvantages:

1. Minimal

These three methods are the only means of transferring your equity from one home to another. You will need to decide which method best suits your situation.

What's an Appraiser Anyway?

By Laura Gater

"People think appraisers are either realtors or bankers. They don't know where to categorize a real-estate appraiser," commented Gilbert Mordoh, SRA, of Gilbert S. Mordoh & Co., Inc., Bloomington, Indiana.

Appraisers aren't realtors. They don't sell homes, nor are they bankers: they don't lend money to buy homes.

Appraisers try to "estimate fair market value for the purpose of the banks, savings and loan institutions and credit unions so that they can determine how much money they want to loan to people," Mordoh said.

Appraisals often help a prospective home buyer determine whether or not a home is worth buying. In a divorce settlement, an appraisal may be useful in order to divide assets equally, according to Mark Figg of First Appraisal Group in Bloomington, Indiana.

Appraisers do, however, work closely with realtors and bankers.

"Appraisers and real estate sales people work very closely together and cooperate in trying to determine fair market value...We try to help the client who's selling, as well as the buyer. Typically, they want to sell the property at fair market value. Realtors in this area do a very good job of that," said Mordoh.

Three basic approaches are used to determine fair market value.

The market approach basically is a comparison of the subject property to others similar to it that have recently been sold, and adjusting for differences (in size and age, for example).

The cost approach is an estimation of reproduction costs of the subject home (new) minus any depreciation that may have occurred since the subject home was built.

The income approach focuses on the potential future income of the subject property, if it is to be used to produce income (such as an apartment building).

Market, cost, and income approaches are used to make adjustments on the subject value. But there's a lot more work involved in determining the value of a home.

"When we go inspect a house, we may only be at the house for 15 to 20 minutes taking measurements and exterior pictures, but there's a lot more background inspection that the homeowner doesn't see," said Mordoh. "People ask me when I finish measuring a house, 'How much is it worth?'"

Appraisers use the standard "Uniform Residential Appraisal Report." This is the report that the banks receive. It includes a neighborhood analysis of such things as convenience to employment, convenience to shopping, convenience to schools and adequacy of public transportation. These are rated by the appraiser as either poor, fair, average, or good.

An exterior description of the foundation, roof surface, window type, gutters and downspouts also is included in the report, along with a brief inspection of the roof, ceiling, wall and floor insulation. A list of kitchen equipment is included, too.

An "improvement analysis" category includes a rating of poor, fair, average or good for such items as closets and storage, energy efficiency, condition of improvements, room sizes and layouts. A sketch of the subject property's' layout is also included in the report.

Appraisers must also research the subject property's legal lot size and taxes to include on the appraisal report.

There are things homeowners can do to improve the appraisal value of their home.

Buyers are willing to pay the extra money for a house that's better maintained," said Figg. "Cleanliness and maintenance are important."

Mordoh added that painting and cleaning nearly always add value to a home, while built-in pools do not necessarily do so. Central air conditioning, landscaping, a modernized kitchen and the location of the property almost always benefit the market value of the home, according to Mordoh.

Any needed repairs, modernization or other inadequacies in the subject property also are noted on the appraisal report.

The subject property is then compared to three other recently sold properties that are very similar to it and that may be in the same neighborhood. Dollar adjustments are made in the comparison of the four properties, either reducing the value of the subject property, or increasing it if it has some additional value or amenity the others do not have such as air conditioning or a deck.

Appraisers, realtors and bankers all work together to help their clients purchase a home. All are crucial to the home-buying process and strive to make the process work for, not against, homebuyers.

Ten Steps to Hiring a Home Contractor

By Eileen J. Safran

It's time to renovate your home!   Remember, every home improvement situation is unique. However, the process of hiring a qualified contractor to successfully complete a job to your specifications is the same in most instances.

Take a moment to review the following ten steps. Utilizing this information will assist in segregating the reputable contractors from the alleged scam artists.

1.   Obtain recommendations from friends.

2.   Interview the prospective contractors in person. Request two names of clients from each contractor.

3.   Visit these completed jobs. Do not accept photographs as proof.

4.   Question the former customers of the contractor regarding specific work habits. Address such topics as:

       a. Was the job completed on time?

       b. Were the workers competent?

       c. Was the contractor available to answer questions or correct any mistakes?

       d. Was the finished project what you wanted?

5.   Check background of candidates with local Better Business Bureau, Attorney General's office, and various licensing bureaus. They will inform you of any complaints which have been lodged against the contractor.

6.   Request written bids from each contractor. Each bid should be easy to understand.

7.   After making your selection, request copies of professional licenses.   Check name on professional license against the contractor's driver's license to make certain that the licenses actually belong to that contractor.

8.   Set up a payment schedule with the winning candidate. Try to withhold at least ten percent of

the cost until ten days after job is completed. This will allow time to identify any defects.

9.   Final contract should contain a clause which forbids any substitution of materials without your permission.

    10.   Negotiate in advance a written warranty for the work to be performed.